PERSUASION

The Complete Psychologist's Guide to Highly Effective Persuasion and Manipulation Techniques – Influence People with NLP, Mind Control and Human Behavior Psychology

Table of Contents

INTRODUCTION

"The only real power available to the leader is the power of persuasion."

– Lyndon B. Johnson, 36th President
of the United States

The ability to connect is an essential trait for daily living. Connecting through communication is a successful way to accomplish what you want throughout your day. Communication is a skill that you need to improve and foster consistently.

A large portion of my day as a psychologist requires me to use a variety of communication skills with clients. Many of the conversations were typical day-to-day connections, but occasionally, it was more high-risk than that. When it is necessary, I found turning to the power of persuasion a powerful tool to persuade someone; to guide them through reasonable argument or discourse. The communication is graceful and delicate. When it is employed correctly, it can deliver immense guidance to others.

Persuasion is an art that intrinsically motivates people to change their behaviors, both in thought and action. This is not a form of manipulation or deception. It is a natural action without force. Having a cheering squad on your side as you strive for success can be achieved through persuasion in both the important and daily conversations. Use this technique to help those around you see what you are aiming for and how they can help you achieve success. Thankfully, persuasion and other communication techniques can be learned and implemented with time and dedication. Become able to influence people in any setting with this one set of skills.

This book is a guide on how to use persuasion to control your own mind and influence others daily. I have used my experience as a psychologist to explain how persuasion has been used in various scenarios that I have encountered, both professionally and personally. The important aspect of persuasion is that influence is easy, but correct influence, or guiding influence, is a talent. If your goal is to get people to actually listen to you, know that this is different than just hearing you; they need to understand you.

Persuasion is a method for getting the outside actions of people to do what you want by "controlling," or adjusting, their inside thoughts. I share my methods to accomplish this throughout this book. These techniques can be used in any scenario. What may come as a surprise is that you are probably already doing many of the persuasive techniques already. This is especially true if you are a naturally compassionate and extroverted person. If you recognize this in yourself as you read along, congratulations, you are already on the path! Now you need to identify exactly what it is that is working, why it works, and how to get even better. For those of you who do not see yourself in the techniques outlined, do not fear. Once you begin putting some of these into practice, you will find it is a natural method of communicating.

The way we behave as humans is very foreseeable. There are personal and societal habits. The way to succeed in life is to understand these repetitions and master the art of mind control with persuasion and influence.

The following chapters are filled with relevant examples, but more importantly, with directions and advice you can follow, not just theories and contemplation. Consider this your go-to manual on how to truly influence others in any situation.

SECTION 1

Program Your Mind:
Understand Persuasion and How to Use It

"You have power over your mind – not outside events. Realize this, and you will find strength."

-Marcus Aurelius

Put yourself in the driver's seat. How? Grasp the concepts of influence, persuasion, and motivation. Why? These concepts will help to deliver to you everything you desire in life. Everyone can employ the rules of persuasion, but almost no one knows what the rules are or how to apply them. For this reason, throughout my revelation of the science and "secrets" of persuasion, you will be able to accurately influence others. Grab life by the horns and enjoy what you want out of life by inspiring others to take action, and revel in the influence you have on other people. Gain the confidence in yourself and earn the recognition of other people's understanding of your way of thinking. Enjoy prosperity, captivate, magnetize, and succeed all through the power of persuasion.

Think of yourself as an incredibly strong magnet and envision people being pulled to you as if they are little pieces of metal that must be brought in by your magnetism. This is what your life will be like when you practice persuasion and influence. This can be used in any aspect of your life: wealth, personal, and professional. Social environments will become a natural playground for you. Doors that were previously closed to you magically begin to be open, and previously hidden paths will be revealed, so you can walk confidently in your direction of success. The principles shared in this book are tried and true concepts that have the power to transform your life forever. Numerous studies of human behavior and persuasion have been used as the foundation for the techniques given to you. They are here at your fingertips; all you have to do is grab them.

This resource guides you with the knowledge of traditional methodologies of persuasion and how to put these leading strategies to use to gain the influence you seek. These methods explain how to make people trust you in a way that takes others decades to establish. Intimidation and fear will no longer have a place in your life as you face the unknown. Now, you can face it with conviction, power, and integrity, every day, in each situation that challenges you. Dominate your fortune.

Persuasion has a power that this world needs. It is formidable and serious. Each time you come in contact with another person, there is an attempt to guide one another or to encourage them to follow your way of thinking. It does not matter who the people are that connect with one another. They could have the same beliefs or different, be the same race or different, have the same career or different. None of that matters. Persuasion is pervasive. The goal is to be trusted, followed, and *heard*. Sometimes this goal can be for good reasons, and sometimes it can be for bad reasons. For the purpose of this book, we are assuming you are here to learn how to persuade in order to improve lives and better yourself and those around you. You want your community to achieve greatness. It is time for you to rise up and uplift those around you during your ascent.

CHAPTER 1.1

Traditional Mental Persuasion

"When I'm getting ready to reason with a man, I spend one-third of my time thinking about myself and what I am going to say -- and two-thirds thinking about him and what he is going to say."

-Abraham Lincoln

Definition and History

Influence is often used interchangeably with the term "persuasion;" however, persuasion is a form of influence and not the other way around. Behavior, motivators, intentions, beliefs, and attitudes can be touched by persuasion in an attempt to influence one or more of those elements. Professional persuasion is often exerted to alter the thoughts of a group regarding something happening and is done so through a variety of means, such as stirring speeches or compelling visuals. Personal persuasion is often used as well in situations like social events. Resources can be used as weapons in the persuasion "battlefield." This means you can use what you have around you, tangible or not, to motivate people to alter their attitudes or behaviors in the manner you want. Sometimes you can use reasoning and logic to persuade, while other times you can use emotion or habit. "Systematic persuasion" is the term applied to logic and reasoning. "Heuristic persuasion" is the term for emotion and habit.

Elocution and rhetoric were the foundations of the Greek's emphasis on persuasion. Both were compelling dynamisms for persuasion. Students learned a copious amount of language to handle the many situations of communication. For example, the ancient Greek trials were determined based on the persuasion of the prosecution or defense in front of an assembly of peers. The speaker was expected to find the correct words and tools to persuade others, and this was true for whatever the circumstance.

Aristotle was the Greek philosopher who was one of the first known people to acknowledge the power and position of persuasion. He recognized its neutrality and its artistic form. He recognized that it could be used for good or bad reasons, but that it stands alone in moral alignment until enacted upon by the speaker. He broke down the necessity of learning persuasion techniques into four logical statements:

1. The speaker is at fault if justice is not served within a court setting. This is because it is the speaker's job to persuade the Assembly. Justice and truth are unadulterated.

2. Teaching is amplified by strong persuasion.

3. Self-defense has no stronger weapon than that of persuasion.

4. In order to fully comprehend a problem, it is important for a strong orator to be able to see all possible choices and contend with any eventual outcome.

Aristotle explained that the main function of persuasion is to explain a person's point of view. He also believed that reasoning and logic bred wisdom and knowledge. Because of this, Aristotle identified three methods of persuasion:

1. *Pathos.* Appealing to the audience's emotions to strengthen a given position

2. *Logos.* Using logic and reasoning to argue about the truth of a given statement

3. *Ethos.* Demonstrating the trust and credibility of the speaker to the audience

Disagreements between human beings are bound to happen, and Aristotle understood it is because people have different perceptions of our world. These perceptions are communicated through dialogue. The challenge was how to tell whose perceptions were correct and most esteemed.

Culture

There are those who believe that being a successful persuader means being pushy or manipulative. They think they will have to force their opinions and ways of thinking onto others. This is an unfortunate cultural belief because it is not correct. Using force and manipulation may garner quick results and short-term success, however, gaining long-term influence requires more natural persuasion. This continuous influence is an implementation of scientifically based strategies carried out with integrity. They are not done with calculated tactics, intimidating others, or deceptive maneuvers. When persuasion is used to communicate truth and good intentions, people instinctively want to be persuaded by you, trust you, and believe in you. Basically, whatever you want them to do, they will do it and will do it happily.

Everyday life requires persuasion, and because of that, the discussion and cultural understanding of it changes day by day. Sometimes the conversation is misunderstood, as explained above.

Being capable of persuasion and yet not being persuaded oneself, is an evolutionary necessity and is important in everything from basic survival to cultivating wealth and success. Different cultures may require different methods of persuasion. This difference is in both how the methods of persuasion are effective and how often they are used. To provide a short example of this, advertisers will adjust the values proposed in the message depending on the culture it is being communicated to. A brand may emphasize a community-based product that brings people together in one country and emphasize individual success in another.

In the mid '90s, two researchers developed a concept called the Persuasion Knowledge Model. This concept provides a structure for analysis of the knowledge of persuasion. It also provides a method for gathering this knowledge.

> *"(It is necessary to include) the relationship and interplay between everyday folk knowledge and scientific knowledge on persuasion, advertising, selling, and marketing in general."*

The method for communicating to the majority of people is to mix colloquial dialogue with scientific findings. This way, the general public can be educated regarding new forms of persuasion through their already established beliefs or common sense. Persuasion proficiency can become muddled when there is consistent mixing of science and folklore. The significance of proficiency can be inferred through communication like the title of a job position, scholarship accolades, or celebrity. This is how we have come to the cultural understanding that used car salesmen are not to be trusted. They are reported to use overt techniques that lead to distrust in our general culture. These techniques can range from giving the keys of the car to the customer before they have bought it to alter their perception of reality, to intertwining their personal life to the customer during the sales process.

Common Theories

There are several theories researchers have developed over the years to explain and apply persuasion to everyday life. Below are a few of those theories and a brief explanation of each one:

Attribution Theory

Human actions can be clarified by one of two attributions, situational or dispositional.

- *Situational.* This has also been referred to as "external" attribution. According to this provenance, there are certain things outside of a person's control that impact their behavior. For example, claiming a person cannot be held responsible for the situation they are in because it was bad before they became embroiled in it, is an application of situational attribution.

- *Dispositional.* This has also been referred to as "internal" attribution. The premise of this attribution is that human actions can be explained by a person's disposition, motive, traits, or abilities. For example, claiming because a person lacks certain knowledge or has a particular personality trait, such as greed or laziness, that is the reason for the current state of affairs, is an application of dispositional attribution.

Another person's behavior is most often explained or sought to be understood by dispositional attribution rather than situational. This is true because we often do not fully grasp the external or outside situaitons surrounding a person, so we gravitate to the complexities of the individual's internal situations. When you are trying to explain yourself or seek for others to understand you, most people will try to persuade others by using dispositional attribution to highlight their achievements and positive behaviors and situational attribution to explain their negative behaviors and inadequacies.

Conditioning Theory

Direct commands are not the actions of a strong persuader. Instead, the aim is to guide people to take their own actions. This is part of conditioning, which is a major part of persuasion. Linking a positive motivation or value to a logo of a company is an example of conditioning. Over time, the messages of joy, sexual desire, or personal connection are shown within the logo. It is an attempt to connect with the audience. Another example is in political campaigns. If a candidate makes direct face-to-face contact with potential voters, and that contact is positive, that voter is more likely to vote for that candidate. We are also conditioned to associate a certain smell or sound with an item. Think of your grandmother's house. If she was fond of baking apple pies or having rose-scented potpourri, later in life, when you smell one of those smells in an unconnected event, you will think of her. You link this with a positive emotion. This is established over time and many exposures to the message, however subtle or overt it may be.

Cognitive Dissonance Theory

Introduced in the '50s, this theory claims that humans want their thoughts, attitudes, and beliefs to be regular. Despite wanting this regularity, our cognitions can swing from alignment to disparity, or between. The disparity between your beliefs, thoughts, or attitudes is called "dissonance." This makes us uncomfortable and feeling as if we are missing something. For example, when you are diabetic and understand that eating excessively sugary foods is bad for you but do it anyways, you suffer from cognitive dissonance. Our natural inclination is to bring this dissonance into synchronization within our mind. We can bring our mental cognitions into alignment. Leon Festinger, the founder of this theory, identified four methods for creating consistent mental processes. These four steps are:

1. *Change.* Our attitude, beliefs, or thoughts need to be changed.

2. *Reduce.* The importance of a thought or belief needs to be condensed.

3. *Increase.* The difference between the dissonance needs to be minimized, bringing the two sides closer to one another.

4. *Re-evaluate.* A negotiation of the reward versus cost of the cognition needs to be reconsidered.

This means the diabetic can change their habit of eating sugary foods, reduce the impact on their health, decide they are not really at risk while eating these foods, or decide the cost of being healthy is not worth giving up the reward of the sugar-laced treat.

Functional Theories

Functional theorists attempt to understand how different situations impact the dissonance of someone's attitude regarding different objects or situations. A function that is impacted by communication can be influenced by persuasion to various degrees. Once a person is persuaded another action would fulfill the function better, the persuasion was a success. Attitudes typically have four main functions:

1. *Knowledge.* Control and understand your life by setting rules and standards that will manage your sense of self.

2. *Value-expressive.* We exhibit a version of ourselves that we want to align with who we want to be or what we want to

believe. This exhibition gives us pleasure because it is aligned with our concept of ourself.

3. *Ego-defense.* People attempt to protect their own egos from personally threatening thoughts or negative impulses. We create processes to keep ourselves from experiencing these negative scenarios.

4. *Adjustment.* Decrease costs and increase affirmative exterior rewards. We choose to move from punishment to rewards with our behavior.

Inoculation Theory

This theory is just like the idea of giving a vaccine to prevent an illness that could invade the body. It may never happen, but by introducing a small amount of the virus, your body creates a defense against the disease, so if it does attack, you are prepared to fight it. To apply this to life situations, consider political parties. They may introduce an easily debunked argument to create the ability for their followers to ignore or dismiss a larger, stronger, or more developed argument from another party. Think about those negative advertisements. One political party may refute the claims of another so that when that opposite party makes those claims, the followers disregard them immediately.

Social Judgment Theory

We attempt to understand persuasive communication by sorting it subconsciously and reacting to it according to our own feelings. The attitude we already have determines how we compare and evaluate new information. This is our anchor point, or initial attitude. From this point, we decide if the persuasion falls into a realm we could accept, cannot accept, or one for which we have little interest. The closer the persuasion falls to their anchor point, the more acceptable it feels to the person.

CHAPTER 1.2

Putting It into Practice

"It takes tremendous discipline to control the influence, the power, you have over other people's lives."

-Clint Eastwood

Persuasion can be used through several various types or principles of action. Different kinds of persuasion can influence people in a variety of ways. Some people are not persuaded by emotional appeals, but rather deal with factual evidence, honoring only what can be seen and heard. On the other hand, others are driven by emotions and do not appreciate factual arguments but are willing to be persuaded with an appeal to the senses. This chapter is going to introduce some of the different types of persuasion and how to use these principles on the various people you will encounter. This chapter also introduces aids for persuasion that will help you influence others and guide them to see your point of view.

Three main types of persuasion are: "appeal to emotion," "appeal to reason," and "appeal to character." These appeals are based on Aristotle's concepts of Logos, Pathos, and Ethos.

Appeal to Emotion

How a person feels can dictate how they decide to take action. It is not based on proof or evidence. If you need to persuade a large group of people, appealing to their emotions can be more effective than using reasoning. This is because the collective population tends to be led by their emotions instead of by logic. This can be seen in examples of entire countries or civilizations making a decision based on emotion rather than logic. Faith or tradition can cause people to become emotional and make decisions for the good or detriment of their society. Imagination and pity are other emotional forms of persuasion that can be used to get someone to align with your way of thinking.

Think of the last time you test drove a car. The sales person wanted you to feel what it was like to drive behind the wheel of that exact car, so you would become more emotionally connected to it and want to repeat that feeling. Pity can be used when they are "honest" about needing the sale that month. Seduction is used in various scenarios and is most evident in forms of advertising. Think about the tagline, "There's nothing that comes between me and my Calvins."

Tradition also plays a role in persuasion. The lines, "This is the way it has always been done" or "If it isn't broke, don't fix it" or "We keep doing what we do because it is how we have always done it," are examples of this mentality. People feel that it is easier to do this than choose another method that may be available to them. Another form of tradition is considered the "bandwagon." This term is often applied to sports fans who choose to support a team because it is the popular choice at the time. You can see this type of persuasion when someone makes a comment like, "Nine times out of ten, people will choose XYZ."

Concluding an argument with an appeal to emotion is a technique that has been suggested for centuries. It reaches a person on an intimate level in order to persuade them to see your point of view. One way to conclude is with a rhetorical question that is not supposed to be answered, but rather appeals to the listener's emotional state. Think about the question, "Why wouldn't you want to feel more secure or happy?" At face value, it may appear to be an appeal to reason, but, in reality, it is to solicit an emotional response to the thought of not being secure or happy. It is an emotional persuasion technique because it does not ask the listener to actually answer the question. Images are another great way to appeal to emotion. If images are not available or feasible, using diction to describe a picture of what you are appealing to can be almost as effective.

Appeal to Reason

Logic is used in this technique to present an argument. Science and founded principles are cited. When someone is demanding proof of something, this is the best method to use. If an argument is based more on faith or feeling, people are less likely to accept it than when there is something tangible they can relate to. Scientists and mathematicians typically work in a fact-based field and make many decisions based on their observations. If you are trying to persuade them of your way of thinking, it would be best to use persuasive arguments based on fact. In addition, stating a single observation, such as what you see, is not enough of an argument for those that need an appeal to reason.

The reasoning is not a fight or disagreement. It is not heated or emotional. The argument is methodical, measured, and logical. There are two processes for reasoning: deduction and induction. Deductions are the general principles of your perception, or way of thinking. Induction is the interpretation of the facts that result in the conclusion. The conclusion is the result you are trying to persuade others to accept. Typically, a deduction has two parts: major points, and minor points. Together, these facts present the logical case to the audience.

The information you present should not be lies and should appeal to the inner reasoning of the people you are speaking with. You should aim to be effective and rational. Analytics, science, math, and academics are all good areas to draw from for an appeal. Choosing important people as sources or experts in their fields are other good resources for a reasonable argument. When you make an appeal in this manner, you have now presented a very effective means of persuasion.

Appeal to Character

This is often labeled as a person's "ethos." Through discussion and speeches, a person can be persuaded if the orator appears to be knowledgeable and kind to the listener. The person looking to persuade another must establish their character to the listener, so they can trust them. Trust is the foundation of an appeal to character.

To show that you possess a strong and trustworthy character, you should establish the following perceptions:

1. *You are a reasonable person.*

2. *You are in a position of authority.*

3. *You live your life by a strong code of ethics.*

4. *You care about the welfare of the listener.*

Another facet of appealing to the character is to make yourself appear not as an authoritative figure, but rather as a relatable and average person. Politicians do this by using terms that a typical person would use rather than political jargon.

Other Persuasion Techniques

Some techniques of persuasion are not used as frequently for various reasons. Some of the techniques are not viewed as ethical means of persuasion, while others have gained a negative opinion of the method. These techniques include:

1. *Power plays.* Those in a position of power tend to automatically have followers. If a person thinks someone is powerful, they will respond to their argument more than someone they view as not having authority. Some people use the image of power or pretend to be a powerful person to persuade people to follow their direction. For example, if you are still an entry-level employee, you could pretend to be a decision maker for the company in situations outside the office to gain access to organizations or events that you otherwise would not be invited to.

2. *Subliminal Messaging.* This can also be called "product placement" in movies or television. Having a product in the background of a movie or in the hands of one of the main characters tells the audience that this product is something that the character or this environment would use. The thought is that you will want to be like that person or model your home after that environment and will look to fill it with the product. Also, it is believed that the more people are exposed to a product, the more likely they will choose it when needing to make a decision related to it. Repetition of images or information encourages people to remember the information and believe in it.

3. *Hypnotism.* This method requires training, but it has been shown to persuade people to do numerous things such as quit smoking or reveal their hidden desires. Typically, a person willingly submits to hypnotism; however, while being hypnotized, they are completely surrendered to the persuasion of the hypnotist.

4. *Deception.* Lying and deceiving are methods of persuading people to follow you. "Fudging the numbers" or "only sharing select information" can be forms of deception because you are centering your argument on only "half-truths" and not portraying honestly the whole situation. People setting up pyramid schemes have used this effectively in the past. They set up a system to take people's

money in a dishonest manner and aim to get out before they get caught in their deception.

Persuasion Aids

There are subtle things you can do to help your persuasive argument, whether it is an appeal to emotion or an appeal to reason. Four of the main aids include:

1. *Personality tests.* A simple questionnaire can be filled out by employees, potential customers, or community members to share information such as how people prefer to communicate. For example, some people respond best to e-mails, while others value the connection through the telephone. Some people can be persuaded by a television commercial, while others only look for information when they need to purchase a certain item. Think about car commercials. Some people are convinced by a commercial that they need to trade in their current car for a new make or model, while others are not persuaded until they have determined they need to purchase a new car. This aid can be helpful to shed a light on a person's personality, so you can best present a persuasive argument.

2. *Sales techniques.* Honest sales techniques can be applied to various communication scenarios effectively. It is a tool that should not be dismissed just because some cultures view sales techniques as deceptive. It is true that some aspects are

not as desirable as others, such as only communicating the good points and "ignoring" the negative aspects; however, there are some desirable skills that can be learned over time. Identifying a person's needs and explaining how your view or perspective fulfills those needs can be ethical and very persuasive.

3. *Communication skills.* The stronger you grasp a culture's language, the better opportunity you have to influence them. For example, when you are writing to someone to persuade, and your letter is riddled with spelling and grammatical errors, they are less likely to take your appeal seriously. If you need to convince a room full of employees to follow a new direction that brings you all into unknown territory, but you fail to prepare a speech, you may find yourself stuttering and stammering. If your oration is peppered with "ums" and pauses, people will have less faith in your leadership. To help you improve your communication skills, you could read books, observe messages, and listen to powerful speakers for inspiration.

4. *Body language.* A person with crossed arms gives the appearance of being blocked and not receptive to messages. A person with their hands at their sides with open fists is more at peace and open to discussion. How you present your communication can be as persuasive as what you say, if not more so. Making eye contact, facing your body towards the person you are speaking to, and not fidgeting are all ways

you can position your body to encourage people to trust and listen to you.

NLP or Neuro-Linguistic Programming

In the 1970s, Richard Bandler and John Grinder developed an approach labeled NLP, or Neuro-linguistic programming. The concept was founded on the understanding that there is a link between the mind, language, and behavior of people. Changing one of these links can alter a person's ability to achieve their goals. This is because we observe our world subjectively. This means that we base "real" events according to our perception of what has happened rather than what has truly occurred. This perception is through our senses and the communication presented to us. Behavior is a response to these senses and perceptions. This means that simply changing the response to the perceptions and senses can change behavior. These responses can be both conscious and unconscious, and we need to learn how to train ourselves to respond differently to scenarios. This change of response is done through conditioning, often where a person is guided through a sequence or steps to come to a different conclusion or behavior. This concept has been applied to all sorts of behavior from smoking or addiction to common, everyday behaviors.

In order to use NLP to influence another person, there are certain steps that need to be taken:

1.   Establish a rapport with the other person.

2. Gather information about the person's current state and where they want to go.

3. Utilize tools and techniques to intervene and alter perceptions.

4. Involve the proposed solutions in the client's life.

Rapport is established through verbal and nonverbal cues like mirroring a person's behavior or mannerisms. Body language is crucial at this stage. Once the rapport is developed, questions are asked to gather the information. These questions have both a verbal and nonverbal response that must be observed. Also, the other person needs to think beyond just obtaining their goal. They need to consider what will happen when they reach that goal. They need to consider both the positive and negative implications of their relationships when they reach their destination. Once the other person has decided this is still the direction they want to go, various persuasion techniques are used to change a person's conscious and unconscious responses, so they can obtain their goals. The final step is to create a way for the person to then experience what it is like when they have achieved that goal. This allows them to feel that success even before it has happened.

CHAPTER 1.3

The Six Truths of Persuasion

"To be persuasive, we must be believable; to be believable, we must be credible; to be credible, we must be truthful."

-Edward R. Murrow

Robert Cialdini is considered one of the most influential authors on the power of influence. He was an intelligent professor who shared his insights with not just those around him but anyone willing to pick up a book and read. One of his books, *Influence,* published in 2006, is most relevant to this chapter. Throughout the book, he conducted his own research and developed six principles of influence.

The six principles he identified are based on the understanding that people can and will be influenced. It is then our job to know what and how to create that influence. The six principles are reciprocity, commitment, social proof, authority, liking, and scarcity. Understanding these principles is helpful, but what truly improves your influence is knowing how to apply them. The following sections of this chapter will identify each one and expound on how to apply them in real-life situations.

The Six Principles

Reciprocity

The premise of this principle is that when you do something nice for another person they will want to do something nice for you. It is to return the favor. This is a natural response. Even without saying it, the person on the other end of your generosity feels like they owe you. They want to pay you back for your consideration.

Commitment

When a person makes a commitment to something, no matter how big or small, they want to keep that commitment. This is especially true if the commitment is a personal one. Many times, this is because the commitments made are aligned with the ideal self-image of the person. The choice to change a behavior or thought process must align with how a person sees themself or wants to see themself.

Social Proof

People follow what those around them are undertaking. It can be small, like repeating a behavior of others because it has peaked your curiosity, or it can be large, like marching into war for a cause you do not fully understand. With the introduction of the online influence, this concept has expounded greatly. This is why websites have customer reviews and ratings and why many people make their decisions based on that information over other facts provided by the company.

Authority

Those in authority, with good or bad purpose, command influence. Most of the people in our communities are not authority figures and prefer to be led by people they view to have a relevant viewpoint, an effective communication method, and a stand from which to share their beliefs. This is a very powerful principle because of the magnitude of influence on a population.

Liking

Being liked by people not only makes us feel good, but it also means we wield incredible influence over those people. To be liked, most people have an inclination to smile and say friendly things. Looks also play a part in this principle. Good looks impact those around them. This may seem biased or unfair, but it is a factor.

Scarcity

People will seek and quickly purchase something if they think it will not be available for long. "While supplies last" or "For a limited time only" are concepts marketing uses to persuade people to take action because of this principle.

Application of the Six Principles

These six principles are what Cialdini introduced, but it is important to understand how to turn principles into actions. Below, each principle is identified with suggestions on how to apply them throughout your daily life.

Reciprocity

Offering something for free, like a professional service or a coffee for a friend, is a simple way to generate reciprocity. Here are some ideas on what to give away:

- Time. Give advice, offer to help with a task, or schedule a time for a phone call to listen to them.

- Knowledge. Help people around you by sharing your expertise on a subject. Give them the information that they need to know.

- Gifts. If you are a business, give away a sample of something to fulfill a need of the customer. If you are applying this on a personal level, give a useful gift to someone like a household item. Be considerate with the gift.

- Content. With the dawn of the internet, it has now become easier than ever to give away free content like printable forms and images, webinars, or books. Tangible content can be given as well in the form of actual books or pamphlets.

Commitment

The first step of commitment is to establish consistency or the concept of advancing your ideal self-image. To create this, it is important to understand who the other person is. Learn about how they view themselves and who they want to be. The messages you present to this other person is then biased and based on their self-image. The next step is to encourage commitment. This is a call to action. Even a small action of a person can lead to larger commitments later down the road. Here are some examples of how to ask for a small commitment:

- Social media following. This is a small connection and commitment. Gain more exposure to your brand if you are a business or to your own image if you are seeking to gain personal influence.

- Watch a video. Choosing to spend their time on watching something you have prepared for them is a small commitment and a non-threatening way to engage a person.

- Fill out a form. Giving information is a commitment to follow-up and discuss something further. Giving someone a phone number is a simple commitment. The more information they provide, like other means of communication or their address, the more they are committing.

Social Proof

Following in the footsteps of those around you is an essential community-building tool. There are a few ways people can apply this principle:

- Testimonials. In a professional setting, this is a powerful tool. Honest and personal accounts can be easily used and shared. Personally, when a person shares their experiences with a product or service with their friends, this word-of-mouth can be more influential than any other form of marketing.

- Show off friends, especially those in common with one another. In the age of social media, it is easy to find connections that would otherwise remain under the radar.

Also, if someone thinks you have plenty of connections and influence on the other people around them, they are more likely to follow you.

- Incite dialogue. If you put out content online that generates comments from other people, more people will show interest in the content and in you. The more dialogue that occurs, the better!

Authority

You can usually establish yourself as an expert in an area as simply as proclaiming yourself as an authority. Find your position and define it clearly. Once that is completed, position yourself to be viewed as the expert in that niche. Create content, be present, and gather and give more information. This is the way to grow your position, recognition, and respect. For example, a person who enjoys riding a specific type of bike in a specific terrain can become very good at what they do on that piece of equipment. This person should then share their experiences and continue to practice, learn, and grow. Once they have established this consistently, they can then advise people on this type of bike and ride, and others will listen.

Liking

There are a variety of ways you can encourage people to like you. Some of those methods include:

- Pictures. Having people, more than one, showing their faces in a photograph with you connects people to you in a more human way. They see you as a person who is already liked by others.

- Average voice. Using a normal voice means more people understand you and will pay attention. Avoid jargon and formal diction. Do not use large and unfamiliar words. Also, when you use the first person in your writing, people connect it more personally to you.

- Be social. This means in person and online. Be active and positive. Friendly comments and presence are important and can greatly influence those around you.

Scarcity

Put yourself out there, but then bring it back by making someone feel it is only for a short time. Offer goods or a service, but restrict the quantity or time it is being offered. Some of the ways to provide scarcity include:

- Control the numbers. Cap the quantity of an item being sold. Only order a few in each size. Explain you are only going to give a few examples of something you are talking about.

- Control the time. Give something an ending time or expiration point. For personal conversations, explain you only have a certain amount of time to discuss something.

This concept does not rely on reality. People just need to think there is scarcity, even if there is none, for this principle to work.

Ultimate Influence:

How to Use Conversation to Persuade in Any Circumstance

"Rhetoric may be defined as the faculty of observing in any given case the available means of persuasion. This is not a function of any other art."

-Aristotle

In your personal and professional life, how much do you control the conversations? This is one way to consider your influence over other people. There are four pillars to influence in communication: the power of position, emotional control, topic expertise, and control over the connection.

Your power of position will be one of the easiest ways to have influence. People with more real or perceived power will have more influence. However, people with power tend to talk more than others, interrupt conversations, and force the conversation to go in certain directions, thus damaging the power of their position. A person who controls their power by engaging in meaningful dialogue can be even more influential.

Emotional control is critical. Letting your emotions run your conversation can be detrimental to your influence, but allowing emotion to pepper your argument or persuasion can be powerful. Think about how best to show your passion for your point of view or way of thinking and use it wisely. Sometimes, a well-placed expletive or watery eye can showcase how deeply you feel about what you are speaking about. Sobbing or turning red while cursing is the opposite. No matter how much of an expert you are on a topic, being too emotional can degrade your authority quickly.

Passion links well with expertise. When a person is knowledgeable and well prepared and also passionate, they are an almost unstoppable force of influence. This is especially helpful if you are not in the position of power in the conversation. It is the terrible truth that experts can be ignored if they cannot communicate their knowledge well, and people with little experience can be followed because they can sway a crowd with a stirring oration. This is another reason why communication is so powerful and needs to be honed.

The final pillar of influence in communication includes controlling the connection. It is not the most powerful pillar, but it is important. This is not just through conversation and verbal information but over your body language and understanding how others are presenting themselves

When you are dedicated to communicating with people, you need to be aware of these pillars of influence and how you can control almost any situation with the correct words or actions. The following chapters are here to guide you in understanding how different conversational tactics can provide you with the ultimate influence in any scenario. Topics such as creating a magnetic personality, how to greet someone and make small talk, and how to listen all lead into understanding how to effectively communicate with others.

CHAPTER 2.1

Magnetism Is Not Magical: How to Create a Magnetic Personality

"Character may almost be called the most effective means of persuasion."

-Aristotle

Many people seek to develop a personality that attracts others to them. This attraction could be for romantic purposes, professional advancement, or personal friendships. The difficult thing about creating this personality is that it requires an honest self-evaluation and mental persuasion. We have internal barricades that we have either intentionally or unintentionally erected that prevent us from developing the connections we are truly seeking. For example, not being able to find the right words in a discussion or feeling uncomfortable speaking with people are types of internal barricades. You need to tear these down so that you can begin improving your conviction.

Those we choose to surround ourselves with also provide a form of communication to others about who we are. When we value ourselves and surround ourselves with others who value themselves, the magnetic and positive energy is apparent. In addition, if you find yourself doubting your greatness, the successful people around you will knowingly or unknowingly encourage you to push yourself to be better. You become more successful, and your personality becomes more "attractive" to others.

To find success with a magnetic personality, you need to overcome low self-esteem and become confident in yourself. Not believing in yourself is crippling and leads to many negative traits. Changing this one area can ultimately change many aspects of your life and draw people to you naturally. This does not mean you need to change who you are, but rather how you view yourself as you are.

Once you accept your unique traits, you will begin to grow in confidence. You should not fear or regret being who you are and instead should seek out the magnetic qualities you already embody. Ask yourself what makes people speak or interact with you. This could be in any situation. Identify situations or scenarios where people spoke and listened to you and why they did so. One of the most common scenarios where people will listen to you and seek you out is when you get them to speak for themselves, and they feel good. People associate feeling good and value with speaking to you and, therefore, want to be around you all the time. They like that feeling and want more of it! Then, when they speak about you to others, they are in turn letting them know how you make them feel. Now, others want to meet and interact with you.

What are some of the practical tips on how to create this connection and get others to feel you are listening to them? How can you make them feel good about themselves? Follow a few of these tips and you will begin to see almost immediate magnetism:

1. When someone you know puts something out there in the world, such as a book, a blog post, or a photograph, you can easily make him or her feel good by offering a thoughtful comment or review. This is especially effective if the person is new at their public endeavor. It is a quick and easy way to show you care about what they are doing and value their contributions.

2. Sending a personal note to someone, either by mail, email, or text, letting someone know how they have impacted your life can make a large impact. It makes that person feel good about their connection to you, and it makes them want to do something nice for you in return.

3. Friendship can be taken for granted, and we often forget to thank our friends for being a meaningful part of our world. A simple show of gratitude can mean a lot to someone, especially when most people are caught up in the excess information prevalent in our communities. This is a social relationship that is often taken for granted. Again, surrounding yourself with positive and valuable friends raises you up and draws even more success to you. This relationship should always be fostered.

4. Do not underestimate the impact of social media. Many people participate on social sites like Facebook and Instagram to receive positive feedback. Writing something kind and thoughtful to someone on these sites outside of the traditional birthday wish is not only validating to them but to all those that view them as a friend. The positivity that you share can become contagious, and others will want you to share some of that consideration with them. They will seek your comments.

5. Choose your compliments well. Do not say something nice if you do not mean it; however, seek to find something

special to compliment a person on. Also, do not offer a compliment and use it to expect something in return. This is evidently insincere. Be honest and thoughtful in bestowing a compliment on someone, and they will feel valued and positive.

6. Sometimes people talk about energy or vibes, and a lot of people may roll their eyes or dismiss this as nonsense; but, the reality is, being positive and enthusiastic in life are apparent to others, even if you never speak to them. When you are confident in yourself and are striving to be a magnetic human, others will notice in your actions, body language, the tone of your voice, mannerisms, and more. These traits will draw others to you subconsciously, just like the opposite traits will repel people.

7. Participate in activities that make you feel good and that involve other people. For example, if you love video games, go to a place that allows others to play video games with you. If you love to run, join a running club. When you are having fun and feeling good around others who also love that activity, you are associating them with that feeling of enjoyment, but they are also associating you with that feeling. Think about the first time you accomplished something you have wanted to do or try, such as surfing or water skiing. When you finally stood up on the board or skis, think about the people that were there with you teaching and

encouraging you. That surge of adrenaline and joy are now connected to those people as well as to the event.

53

CHAPTER 2.2

Steps to Making Casual Conversation

"That's all small talk is - a quick way to connect on a human level - which is why it is by no means as irrelevant as the people who are bad at it insist. In short, it's worth making the effort."

-Lynn Coady

The fear of talking to someone you have never met, or know nothing about, can bring up anxiety in even the most confident and outgoing person. But being able to communicate and form meaningful connections is vital to creating happiness and strong human bonds. The thought of surface conversations may not seem to fulfill this desired link; however, it is not fake or a waste of time. This does not mean that you should only talk about unimportant matters like the weather or the food. People seek deeper conversations that are meaningful. This is because we are social and constantly seek meaning. We want our lives to mean something. Getting into this type of conversation is not always stress-free and does not always flow with ease. Think about the last time you were in an awkward conversation with someone when a person you were trying to talk to did not want to or did not seem capable of responding back. Or have you ever felt trapped in a conversation you have no interest in? Having strong small-talk skills can help you turn these situations around and leave you and your communication partner fulfilled and happy.

The purpose of this chapter is to provide a how-to guide for making small talk that is both meaningful and bonding. Break the ice, create new relationships, and grow professionally. The more you practice this skill, the more comfortable you will become with it.

<u>*Step 1: Use body language and a friendly tone to set the foundation of the conversation.*</u>

Sincere eye contact, well-placed nodding, and leaning your body into the other person are all good forms of body language that communicate to the other person that you are engaged and are listening. A polite smile, open arms, and attention are all important. Not having welcoming body language can shut down a conversation before it even starts.

If you can, turn your whole body towards the person you are talking to. Be mindful that this stance and leaning towards them is friendly and does not feel forceful or threatening. Other useful tips include:

1. Put away your cell phone. Do not check your email or messages when trying to connect with someone in front of you. Even just having your phone out can distract from the conversation. Put it out of sight if you can. If you are at dinner or a networking event with a table, do not place it on the table. If you need to keep your phone out because of an important call or email, let the person know that this is the reason for the presence of the phone. This way they know you are not using it as a way to avoid talking with them.

2. Be careful not to seem overly eager. Do not lean in too far that they feel intruded upon. Do not scare them by never breaking eye contact. If you try to talk to someone when you are in their personal bubble, they will reject the conversation instead of wanting to engage in it.

If you know the person you are about to speak with, use their name in a friendly way, such as, "Hi, Tom, it's nice to see you." If you do not know the person, consider another friendly greeting like, "Hi, my name is Alison. What is your name?" When they reply with their name, make sure to use it. Some people suggest finding a way to say it three times in the early conversation, so it is committed to your memory. Use this in conjunction with good body language to make the person feel special and not like a nuisance or a placeholder until others arrive.

Focus on keeping the topics of conversation light, positive, and fun. Try to laugh easily and have a smile ready at a moment's notice. This is relevant even if you have had a bad day. This person is not a close confidant yet, so it is best to not overwhelm them or shut them out by being negative. Negativity turns most people off immediately, especially when they do not know you.

If you struggle with what to say after the initial greeting, offer a sincere and unique compliment followed by a question about it. For example, "Wow, you have a stunning pair of earrings. What a beautiful accent piece to your outfit. Where did you find them?" This is especially great if you want to direct them to a topic of shopping, but it can just simply open the door to a conversation. It opens the door with grace because it makes the person feel appreciated and noticed. If you do not want to introduce yourself first, you can start with the compliment and then move into a friendly greeting.

Step 2: Begin the conversation on common ground and without saying much.

Now that contact has been made, you can begin actually speaking to one another. There are a few different ways you can start this conversation beyond those first few introductory remarks. For example, you can find out if you have something in common with the other person. This can be about anything, big or small. It is okay to begin small here. Weather can be a good introduction as long as it leads to topics that matter to you and the other person. Think of comments like, "Don't you think this presentation is so informative?" or "Wasn't that snow storm this afternoon so crazy?" or "This restaurant serves the best bacon." Once you gain a link to common ground you can then move forward by exposing something about yourself.

This is an intimate gesture that lets the other person drop their guard a bit. Do not feel you need or should share something too personal. That will backfire on your intention of connection. Instead, try something like, "I have actually been coming to these sessions for years now and always find out something new." or "I was trying to go to the gym to work out today but had to try to do some things at home instead. It was awful!" or "Every time I come to this restaurant I order an extra side of it to take home for the next day. It's like treating myself to another breakfast out but in the comfort of my PJs."

Once you have demonstrated that you are willing to share personal information about yourself, you should invite the other person to add to the conversation. This is the time to ask a lot of questions, but remember, steer clear of "heavy" topics. This is meant to be a light and fun conversation. Things like religion or politics can get somber quickly and negate the purpose of the small talk. When you ask your questions, keep them open-ended, meaning you are phrasing them in a way that encourages the person to respond with a sentence rather than a yes or a no. Typically, open-ended questions begin with a "why" or "how." "What" questions tend to garner short and simple replies. Aim to grow the conversation with the questions you ask rather than narrow it down.

Other questions to avoid are the typical ones like, "What do you do?" or "Where are you from?" These are stock questions and do not show the interest you have in the other person. Be curious about them and try to build on the common ground you found earlier. Do not ask "How was your day?" but rather "Did anything exciting happen to you today?" or "What happened in your day today?" Once the person is talking, listen to what they have to say and ask more questions about it. Be interested!

Following the above examples regarding an information session, snowfall, or bacon, follow up questions can be, "Have you come to other sessions, or is this your first time? The others I attended were good, but this one has been really great!" or "Did the snow keep you from doing anything this afternoon?" or "What do you come to this restaurant for? Is it for the bacon, too, or for the awesome coffee?"

These all seek to expand on the common ground and ask the other person to provide their own opinions in a safe conversation.

Another form of engagement can be to ask for advice. Many people love to talk about themselves and what they have done. It makes the other person feel good and validated. Asking advice can sound like, "Have you attended other programs outside of this company? What are your thoughts on how this one is presented?" or "How do you get in a workout when you are home-bound? I struggle with staying motivated and focused," or "Do you have other favorite restaurants in the area? I'm always on the hunt for other great options!"

After you initiate the engagement and response from the other person, you need to decide how you will respond to keep the conversation expanding and going. This means, after the person responds to your initial question, you need to ask another question or reply with your own statement. Sometimes a well-placed and appropriate joke can be relevant. Be careful with jokes. Keep them politically correct and light-hearted. "Dad" jokes like silly knock-knock jokes or puns can be good in your communication repertoire. Also, be cautious with the questions you are asking. Do not make the other person feel like they are in an interrogation. Keep sharing bits about yourself with the conversation, so it is a true dialogue, back and forth.

Think about your response as a natural inquisition or connection. You could respond something like, "That is awesome you have been able to attend so many other great programs. What was your favorite one?" or "That sounds like a great method for working out at home. How did you discover that? Do you follow someone or something online?" or "I have tried that restaurant as well. Some people claim it is a little stuffy, but I do not agree."

Once the conversation begins going back and forth, observe what is around you, including more of the other person. This could be something they are wearing or something within the room that you think would apply to both of you. This way if the topic at hand wears out, you can have something lined up to introduce next.

Most of the banter should be back and forth, with you inquiring and the other person talking. Try to do more of the listening and less of the talking. Asking the person, "Tell me more," is like a magic bullet to open up the other person and get them sharing. This also allows you to sit back and really listen. Remember to watch their verbal cues to make sure they are still engaged in the topic and conversation. Rephrase the conversation of the other person and reflect on the comments to show you are truly paying attention. When replying to their questions, share details, not just surface information. This gives the other person personal information to work with as well.

When you actually listen to the other person's comment, you may pick up on other common grounds you could use to steer the conversation towards. Be careful not to take over the conversation and change the topic without waiting for an appropriate time to do so. For example, when someone responds to your question by saying, "I live in downtown New York because I love the West Side. The energy there is addictive." You could respond with, "That is why I chose to live in the heart of my city as well; there is nothing like the bustle of all that activity. My favorite thing to do is to watch people walking down the sidewalk and imagine what they do for work or where they are going." This allows the other person to elaborate on your comment or share more about what energy they like in their neighborhood.

Step 3: Bring the conversation to a close with grace and a follow-up plan.

As you recognize the conversation is nearing an end, like when the music is about to start, the break is coming to a close, or the event is ending, make sure you have shared something personal about yourself. This means something you are passionate about but nothing that is too much for a first conversation. Those more sensitive topics can wait until a deeper bond has been developed. In a small talk connection, you want the person to feel they have connected and not been filler for a time slot.

If you are interested and feel the connection was good, you can mention getting together again. It is not inappropriate to tell the other person that you enjoyed talking with them about the topics you covered and would like to talk more. Ask for their contact information. If you do not feel comfortable, encourage or mention a place you both visit for the opportunity to meet again. Try phrasing things like, "I am really looking forward to that movie premier and would love to go with someone who is equally as excited. Can I get your number, so we can go together?" or "It is so refreshing to meet someone who loves bacon as much as I do. I like to host a potluck once a month and would love for you to come to try some of the different concoctions we come up with, and for you to share your own. Can I get your contact information, so I can send you the details?" or "Maybe I'll see you at the coffee shop in the neighborhood sometime. I hear they are doing a story time on Tuesday mornings. It would be fun for our kids to get together while we grab a cup."

Finish the conversation clearly and thoughtfully. Let them know you loved speaking with them, wish you could talk longer, or you want to introduce them to another person you think they would connect with.

CHAPTER 2.3

It All Starts with 'Hello'

"You've probably noticed how when someone says hello or smiles at you, your automatic reaction is to say hello or smile back."

-Shawn Achor

Why Should You Smile?

Emotions are powerful motivators. People make decisions based on their emotions most of the time. For example, if someone feels nervous about something, they will be more aware of how they handle themselves or things around them. They may place more importance on seemingly unimportant things. On the other end, you do not always know how someone is feeling until you talk to him or her. That first impression of you can either lower or heighten the emotion of the other person. The difference between making a meaningful connection with someone and creating a gap between the two of you can boil down to this first contact. The best way to create a positive first impression? Smile. And then say, "Hello."

People become more comfortable when they are greeted with a friendly smile. If the greeting can be personal, it can go even further to calming someone down or cheering them up. The greeting can be personalized by simply adding their name. It can be personalized further by adding a unique compliment to them or engaging in small talk that is based on common ground between you and the other person. Make the person the center of attention as quickly as possible. This helps you build trust and rapport.

Another component is the tone of your voice. Be congenial and kind. Mean what you say when you say hello. Do not write off this powerful moment of connection as unimportant. Make it powerful with importance. Enjoy the contact and camaraderie.

Saying hello to someone is not a burden. It is a common contact that we do on a daily basis with all sorts of people. It is a natural part of communication. This is why it should be done sincerely and with thought. It is also why it is one of the simplest methods of showing your earnestness. How can you do this easily? Smile. And then say, "Hello."

To be ready to greet people in such a friendly and cheerful manner, it is important to be prepared mentally for this task. This means being in a good mood. If you are not, or are experiencing bad circumstances, try to put yourself in a happy place by thinking of a positive experience or memory before you know you will be meeting another person. Before you interact with another person, take a deep breath and think positive thoughts. This calm and positive nature will come through in your facial expressions and tone of your voice. The people you meet will feel comfortable and trusting.

If the outside situations or your mood are too bad, and you cannot change into a positive attitude, pretend like you have. Plaster a smile on your face despite how you feel. It can sometimes be effective and influence the environment around you. It has also been proven to improve your own mood.

Saying hello with a bright smile can transform a client who only purchases every now and again into a loyal regular, turn someone's mood from sadness or frustration to a brighter outlook, and diffuse a tense situation between people. Recognize this power and feel it when someone smiles and says hello to you. It is not a magic bullet. It is a natural trait that we can use to make a major influence at the start of any connection.

Why Should You Say Hello?

The greeting is a powerful tool that jump-starts a good conversation. It opens the door to a personal connection which all humans need. The friendly greeting of a "Hello" and a smile can put a stranger at ease and set the connection up for success. The first impression you make on someone will be dependent a lot on your greeting. The same goes for your first impression of them!

A greeting can be considered an introduction to a large group of people as well as to an individual. When you are giving a speech, that first minute of your talk sets the tone of your influence. It captivates the people's interest and attention. The opinion of your speech from these people will rest on how well you do in that first minute of your greeting and introduction.

When someone knocks on your door or calls you on the phone, people expect you to greet them because it is considered common courtesy. It does not matter who the person is that calls or stops by. You are expected to greet them with a friendly greeting. In fact, when the phone rings or the doorbell sounds, we often drop what we are doing, no matter if we are in the middle of something or not, and rush to greet that person. This expectation of attention and kindness should be a common courtesy in all your greetings.

A thoughtful, personal greeting that makes the other person or people feel special is valid because those people are important. They should be treated as such. Think of a customer to your business. They are literally funding your dreams; treat them that way. Think of a friend who is being considerate and stopping by to see you. They are showing you how they care about you and your situation; treat them that way. If you do not greet someone, they feel ignored and neglected. It feels good to at least be acknowledged!

If a greeting is to be the most effective, it should be personal and sincere. There are some key components to making someone feel like they are truly being greeted:

- Wow them right away. The first ten seconds of an interaction can be all you get to make an impression in a personal setting. In a speech to a group of people, you get about 60. If you fail to greet the person with a friendly hello within this time frame, you will have damaged that first impression. This does not mean they will never be won over to your point of view or value you as a friend, but it does mean you have now set yourself up for a more challenging battle of persuasion. If a person feels ignored, they will probably look elsewhere for a conversation or influence.

- Look them in the eye. If you do not bother to look up at someone when you say hello you might as well not even say it. Same goes for addressing a crowd. If you have your head down and are staring at your notes, or your shoes, or are looking over your shoulder, people will feel you are dismissing them and that they are not worth the common courtesy of a proper greeting. They feel disrespected. Lifting your head, bringing your eyes to focus on them, and having a soft and friendly gaze go a long way in making a person feel validated.

- Do not forget to smile. If you say hello to someone without a smile, even if it is fake and they know it, they will feel this greeting is just a requirement, and you do not care about them. A fake smile is better than no smile, even though it does not pack the same punch. This component of the greeting is so important that it warrants its own section in this chapter! Pair a cheerful "Hello" with a smile and you have now established a strong introduction.

- Make it personal. Using someone's name when you know it makes a person feel like they belong in that conversation and that they are special. Hearing your name, in a personal or professional setting, is something most people love to hear. In addition, recalling something about them, such as a funny story, a common purchase, or a previous action, can go a long way in establishing the feeling that you care about them and value them as a person. If you forget someone's name, you can get around this by using phrasing like, "It's good to see you again." This makes the person still feel like you recognize them despite not being very personal.

- Mix it up. If you say the same thing to everyone all the time, people will catch on quickly that you are not really paying attention to them. The first couple of encounters you may be able to get away with, but people will eventually realize you are not being sincere. Using your observations, customize your greeting to the person you are talking to. For example, if the AC is out in the auditorium of people you are addressing, acknowledge that by saying, "Good afternoon, thank you to everyone who is here today. I know it is uncomfortable without the air conditioning, and it means a lot to me that you have chosen to stay to listen to my message. Please do not hesitate to get a drink of water throughout my speech to keep yourself cooler." This is a far better greeting than something like, "Good afternoon, thank you for being here." Also, for personal greetings, mix up how you say hello. Think about where the person had to come from to get there, or what is going on that led them to you.

- Do not forget about yourself. People may not already know who you are, or they may have forgotten. By introducing yourself, you let the person know how to address you and drive the conversation to a more personal level, not just a surface interaction.

- Respect the bubble. People have an invisible bubble of personal space. When someone crosses into the bubble, knowingly or unknowingly, it can make him or her feel uncomfortable. It puts them on edge because they view this as an attack on their personal safety, even if it is a friendly contact. A good rule of thumb is to stand about three feet from the other person and only occasionally interact closer than that when necessary. A handshake is not considered an intrusion into the bubble if it is expected. A hug can be too much. An arm around the shoulder or a whisper in the ear can be too intimate for general acquaintances. Give them space.

- The best policy is honesty. If you can, always be sincere in your greeting. Be genuine. When you fake it, especially if you fake it all the time, people will recognize this and be turned off. If you have to fake a friendly greeting, do not be afraid to explain why you are having a hard time briefly. Use a comment such as, "Hi. I'm sorry I'm a little off, I had a rough time getting here, but I am excited to be able to meet you."

When someone perceives you as friendly, and you make them feel special, valued, important, and that they belong, people will want to listen to you and come back to you.

CHAPTER 2.4

How Listening Is a Form of Persuasion

"The art of conversation is the art of hearing
as well as of being heard."

— William Hazlitt, Selected Essays, 1778-1830

Can you distinguish the difference between hearing and listening? Some people think that there is no difference between the two, but being an "active" listener is very different than just observing someone is speaking words in your general area. The concept of "active" listening is an exchange technique where the listener must respond to the speaker by replying to what was said by rephrasing what they heard. It shows that both people understand each other. Each word the person says is heard, and the listener is clear on what has been communicated to them. The listener is not thinking about anything other than what is being said. This listening skill is what builds quality relationships.

Listening to someone when they talk to you is more than just being polite or kind. It holds a lot of weight to the person's opinion of you and how you value them. Listening can also accomplish a lot of things in your efforts to persuade them to see your point of view or to do something different. To be a good persuader, you need to be a good listener.

Why Is It Important to Listen?

The majority of this book has been centered around how to communicate with others to persuade them to follow you, to change their perspective on a topic, or to make them do something different. You use your words and body language to get them on your side and have influence over them. So how does not talking and letting them speak accomplish this? There are a few reasons.

First of all, people trust you more when they feel they can share with you. If a person feels that they can talk openly about things with you and that you will listen to what they have to say, they trust you more. They see that you value their point of view. Trust is the cornerstone to influence and establishing your character. Listening is the easiest method to gain that trust. When a person realizes you are willing to listen to them and you are encouraging them to talk, your credibility goes up. And this is not only with the person you are speaking to, but all the people witnessing the conversation. People want to be heard, and when they see someone is willing to do that, they want to be the next to talk. They see a listener as capable and competent. They view you as wanting to work with them and not against them. You are not telling them how to do something without first listening to how it is being done already. Imagine if someone you are speaking to is upset about something. Simply opening your ears and listening to them can show your empathy and support. They feel they are important enough to be listened to. You subconsciously are telling them that you respect them, and they are important. What a powerful connection!

As a psychologist, the majority of my role is to listen to people. There are many times I do not say more than a few words to people. Yet, despite my silence, my clients trust me and come back week after week. They know I value them and think what they say and do is important. I demonstrate this to them through my listening, not just because I have training in how to help them.

I am able to help my clients by listening to the information they provide me and make mental notes about important details. I can do my job because they gave me a lot of information to work with. The questions I ask or the comments I make are there as a guide to get people to open up and share about themselves. This also encourages them to drop their guard a little bit. If I did not spend the time listening to them, why should they spend the time listening to me?

Think about an exchange with a person recently where you felt they jumped in too soon with their perspective and thoughts. Did you feel engaged, valued, and understood? This could be a friend or colleague or a sales person who does not take the time to listen. Consider how it made you feel when you thought they weren't listening to you. Have you ever asked someone a question, and they seemed to be ignoring you or they did not answer it? Instead of bonding, do you feel disconnected? You cannot get what you need to get done if you do not have a connected audience to listen to you. Listen to them, and they will listen to you.

8 Tips on How and Why to Be a Better Listener

1. People fall into the trap of misunderstanding the power of listening. They do not see the benefit or reward of listening to another person, especially when they have an agenda. But the theory of reciprocity applies to listening. If you show you are actively listening to another person, they will be more

likely to listen to you in return. If you focus on understanding, they will, too.

2. Keep in mind that part of active listening is to be able to recall the conversation and information later to show you understood what was communicated. Stay alert and ask questions or for information to be repeated, so you make sure the information sticks in your mind. This also helps you stay in the moment and stop thinking about what to talk about next. The information that you will recall is powerful. After all, "Knowledge is power." The person talking is giving away information, and the person listening is gaining it. By listening, you are gaining more power.

3. Staying focused on the person is critical. This means keeping your eyes focused on them the majority of the time. Aim to increase the amount of time you make eye contact in conversations and focus on their eyes. When the person feels that you are paying attention to them they feel cared for and understood. This is a valuable feeling to people and something that is not common in today's society.

4. Remove distractions if possible. This includes your phone or computer. Multi-tasking is not possible when you are trying to listen, because you need to be completely present in the conversation. Browsing the internet or reading an email will make you miss some of what the other person is saying, not to mention the negative impact it has on eye contact. If you

need to use it during the conversation to check something or note something related to the conversation, let them know that. For example, say, "That's an interesting question, and I am not sure about that. Let me look it up quickly," or "I need to write that down. That is great insight!"

5. Recall what is said by paraphrasing the information. Just a few seconds to recall some of the main points you just heard not only confirms that you heard the information correctly, but it also shows the other person that you really were listening to them. This gives the other person the opportunity to correct something you said to make sure it is accurate. The summary also sets the tone for sharing your perspectives or questions appropriately. The summary is not an assumption, but rather a confirmation of the information just provided to you. Active listening requires observation but not mind-reading. Do not assume anything based on something the other person said or did. Ask questions to clarify the information.

6. A clear and present mind is needed. Being tired or distracted makes it almost impossible to listen well to another person. Take a walk outside to get some air or do some exercises to keep your mind and focus sharp.

7. Listening can be hard when you want to relate to another person. You want to share your experiences, and sometimes you feel like if you just input a little information about

yourself, the other person will feel more connected to you from this common ground. This is not the case. Do not interrupt or jump in. Do not offer solutions if the person is not asking for them. Do not take over the conversation talking about your situation that was similar to theirs unless they ask. Just listen until they are done talking. Some people just need to vent and do not need a solution. They will probably arrive at it on their own. Let them talk. This also allows you to not share something you wish you had not. You cannot take back information once you say it; use it wisely. Wait until it is the right time to share a common ground or offer advice. It will be more powerful when used thoughtfully later.

8. Know when enough is enough, and you cannot take anymore. If you are tired, stressed, or in a hurry, you need to let the other person know because it will affect your ability to listen to them. If a friend calls you and needs to be heard, let them know that you need to start dinner in 30 minutes, or you have an appointment you need to leave for by 4 PM. Also, if you have been listening and trying to stay present but notice you are starting to wander, let the person know you need to take a break. Maybe use the restroom to decompress or get something to eat or drink. It is okay to step back and process before being a present listener again. There is a reason there is a time limit to psychiatry sessions! Being honest about your ability to listen is better for the

relationship than trying to fake it. Also, by being honest you can prevent yourself from saying something you do not really mean or that is not appropriate. A thoughtless comment can cause irrevocable damage to the relationship.

Show You Are Listening and Not Just Hearing Noise

This is a practice that takes time and effort. Calming your mind and focusing on just the speaker is a challenge when there are so many distractions around us that we cannot control. We also have our own need to communicate and be listened to. If the topic of the speaker is something we do not value ourselves or find interesting, the process of actively listening can be even harder. Avoid the temptation to stop the conversation or change the subject. Practice your skills in any situation, so when you need to use them to gain maximum influence over a person or group of people, you can be effective and persuasive.

It is important to note that active listening is not a stepping-stone to an argument. It is a way to understand another person. If you do not agree with their viewpoint, ask more questions to see why they think or behave that way. The more you understand, the more credible you will be, and when you do begin to use influence over their thoughts or behaviors, they are more likely to follow your direction because you understood them and are speaking to them personally rather than on a surface level. Encouraging them to share upfront allows you to get all the information you need to persuade them without begging for it or trying to get it out of them later.

To show someone you empathize with what they are saying, nod your head. A well placed "Yes" or "Uh-huh" can be a quick way to illustrate that you are listening and understand them. Body language plays an important role in communicating without using words. Other phrases like, "Go on," "Tell me more," "Wow," "Great!" or "Interesting" all show you're listening and interested. To make sure you understood what was said, ask questions that begin with, "What I understand then is that....?" or "So what you are saying is...." or "What I just heard you say is...." or "What do you mean by....?" These are other ways to ask clarifying questions to show that you are listening and to make sure the information you are taking in is accurate.

CHAPTER 2.5

What to Do When People Do Not Listen: How to Handle Conflict

"Conflict is drama, and how people deal with conflict shows you the kind of people they are."

-Stephen Moyer

Conflict is inevitable when you are seeking to understand and persuade others. Different goals, personalities, and opinions all influence how we respond to information, and emotions can cloud judgment. Being able to handle conflict, getting people to listen to you, and communicating with those that disagree with you are all skills that take time to master but are some of the strongest traits you can develop for persuasion and influence.

Resolve Conflict in 5 Steps

When you do get into a disagreement with someone, whether it is a heated argument or a passive disagreement, it is important that you handle it well to keep the relationship intact. Below are five steps you can use to find and resolve just about any disagreement:

1. Find the cause. This means the more information you have about why the conflict began, the better chance you have of resolving it. Ask questions to find out where the disagreement began. Questions like, "When did you begin feeling this way?" or "How did this problem begin?" Encourage people to open up and be honest about how they feel. If you are mediating a disagreement between two people, let each person tell their side of the story without interruption. This lets both parties know that you are impartial to the conflict and want to find an amicable solution.

2. Life does not happen in a vacuum. Understand that just one incident does not lead often to conflict. Typically, there are other factors at play. Something could have happened earlier between the two that has now festered to a boiling point. Or you may have triggered an old wound a person is nursing without realizing it. It is important to look outside and beyond the current conflict to understand what the true cause of conflict is. Questions like, "What do you think caused this to happen?" or "When do you think this conflict first arose?" help you find the root of the issue, not just the conflict at hand.

3. Involve the others in finding a solution. Do not assume you know how to fix a problem, whether it is between you and another person, or between two people you are talking with. Once the person has shared their thoughts on why and how a conflict arose, ask them how they see it being resolved. It may be completely irrational or illogical. It can even still be hurtful language or ideas, but it is important you give the other person the opportunity to offer a solution to fix the relationship. The goal of this is to get the other person to stop being defensive and start thinking about working together. Try asking a question such as, "How can we make this better between us?"

4. Once the other person offers a solution or two, discuss what you think would be an acceptable solution if they did not already mention it. Make sure to summarize the solutions

the other person offered and identify the benefits of each of their solutions. Do the same with your suggestion if you offered one as well. Involve them in the discussion about what would be best for the two of you or the group. Sometimes a solution is not great for either person, but it is the best for the organization or group. It is important to note this and find a way both people can support it.

5. After a solution is identified that both people can support, each person needs to agree on how they are going to move forward after the conflict. Shaking hands typically solidifies this. Asking questions like, "What actions are you going to take to prevent conflicts in the future?" or "What do you plan to do if a conflict arises again?" can help make sure you know how the other person plans on addressing a problem moving forward.

These steps work well with someone who is willing to communicate and listen, but what if they are not open to listening to your point of view?

How to Get Them to Listen

When you are trying to communicate something, maybe a different perspective, instructions, or advice, it can be frustrating when the other person is not willing to listen to you. Despite your best efforts, some people are bad listeners. They may choose to not listen, or they just do not know how to. There are two things you can do in this situation: give up and walk away or keep trying to communicate with them. If you are trying to persuade someone, you need to be able to communicate with them. In order to communicate, they need to listen to you. This means, if you decide you really want this non-listener to be influenced by you, you need to stick it out and find a way for them to communicate with you.

Not all non-listeners are doing it intentionally, and you do need to be patient while they find their way to trusting in your words. Sometimes they need to make a small mistake, so they listen to you before making a large one. Think about children, they often learn by making mistakes. If you provide guidance to them about not jumping off the couch because it can hurt them, they may not listen. When they do hurt their elbow or knee, they will put it together that you were right. This means when you advise them not to jump off from the roof onto the trampoline, there is a stronger likelihood they will listen to you because you were right before, and they did not listen.

There are other times people will not listen and you cannot understand why. Maybe they feel they know more than you, or they do not like to admit they are wrong. Sometimes they are defensive about change or different ideas. In my experience, some of the best ways to deal with people who do not or cannot listen include:

- Ask more questions and get their perspective on the topic at hand. Forcing them to talk about a subject will begin to open them up to a conversation.

- Consider approaching the topic in a different way or with different language. Maybe they do not like the tone of voice you used, or the language was confusing to them. Rephrase what you are saying to see if that engages them better.

- Reflect on how you presented information. Did you sound like you were barking orders instead of providing guidance? Were you acting like a know-it-all instead of a confidant? Adjust if needed.

- Do not dismiss someone's emotions as unimportant. If something you said made them angry or upset, do not belittle them by saying, "You should not be angry." Instead, find out why they feel that way about what you said and explain your stance in a manner that is personal to them.

- Avoid trying to force someone to do or say something. Be understanding of a person's place in the relationship and conversation. Allow them to feel how they feel and think the way they think before trying to alter their perceptions. Applying force is a poor form of persuasion. Guiding them to find the answer on their own typically prevents conflicts and opens doors to communicate.

- Do not underestimate different communication methods. Sometimes, it is not the right time or place to speak to someone about something. They may be busy, stressed, or tired. If they need to be able to revisit your communication, consider writing it down. If you want them to emotionally connect with what you are saying, try involving a visual aid of some sort. Graphs, charts, or pictures can be powerful. If they seem distracted, set a time for them to have the conversation. Setting a time and place aside to talk can be a powerful tool in getting them to listen to you.

- Allow silence to exist. Do not feel the need to jump in and fill a void, especially if you are talking about an important or difficult subject. Some people just need time to think about their response, and your constant speaking can distract or discourage them from trying to engage with you.

- Find a tool to make them more comfortable with you. Think about children and needing a blankie to hold in unfamiliar situations. Provide a "blankie" to the person you are talking to. This could be a favorite snack or drink, a comfortable chair, or an intimate room.

How to Talk to People Who Disagree with You

There will come a time when you need to disagree with someone. Despite all your powers of persuasion, you will need to debate something. Writing a well-crafted argument can seem like the best and most effective approach, but in reality, the best way to persuade someone is in person. This means that they either watch something you have prepared, or you speak with them directly about it. This method of communication makes the other person view your argument as more valid and your character stronger than if you wrote it down. The tone of voice and body language are factors in this interpretation. Also, the written word takes the humanity from you, and opens up the opportunity for the other party to belittle your intelligence or moral character. It may sound harsh, but when emotions come into a disagreement on important topics, this is a subconscious maneuver we all are naturally inclined to.

In order to communicate with someone you openly disagree with, stay visible as much as possible and follow these steps:

1. Use the other person's perspective to begin your conversation. Identify what you disagree on, such as politics or religion, and state what that person's beliefs are. Then use that to discover why they made those decisions. For example, if someone believes gun control is irrelevant, but you think it is important, start with their perspective and find out why they think there should be less control.

2. Take the time to be there in person. This not only makes you more of a "person" to the opposing party, but it shows them that you value the relationship and are showing up to have the hard talk.

3. If you cannot be there in person, be there on their screen. Facetime or Skype them. Videoconference if needed. At the very least, have the phone conversation. Avoid text and writing at all costs and resort to it only when necessary. And finally, do not use social media to disagree with someone. It

may be tempting, but it is futile. It is not effective and typically a waste of time.

CONCLUSION

"At the end of reasons comes persuasion."

- Ludwig Wittgenstein

Thank you for making it through to the end of *Persuasion: The Complete Psychologist's Guide to Highly Effective Persuasion and Manipulation Techniques – Influence People with NLP, Mind Control and Human Behavior Psychology*. Let's hope it was informative and able to provide you with all of the tools you need to achieve your goals.

The next step is to start practicing the skills in this book. Seek out people you do not know to hone your small talk talents. Mentally prepare yourself to sit and listen to what people have to say. Look to disarm disagreements with kindness and understanding. Persuade people to follow your lead with natural grace and poise. Using the techniques and suggestions in this book, you can successfully control people's thoughts and get them to do what you want. Just remember, this power can be used for good or bad reasons. The more influence and persuasion you control over others, the more this responsibility is important. Remain persuasive to the betterment of those around you, and you will not be at a shortage of authority or power.

A successful application of persuasion does not mean you will always experience this win. This also means that a failed attempt does not mean you are never going to enjoy the ability to get people to follow your way of thinking. This is a process and requires training. You must practice to get better and better. The more you communicate with others, the more opportunity you will get to become the persuasive leader you seek to be. Apply this persuasion in your home, with friends, family, or at work. When you are guiding and communicating naturally, you will experience the power of persuasion that has been a part of human nature since the beginning.

Part of this process is to be aware and observant of yourself and others. You must understand what persuasion is, the reason you are seeking to influence another person or group of people, and how you will present yourself and your argument in a manner that gets people to want to listen and follow-up. Of course, there will be those who are resistant or do not want to be persuaded. This just means you get to put those skills to the test and challenge your powers of persuasion. Use the final chapter of this book to remind you how best to deal with those who conflict or disagree with you, or who just plain refuse to listen to what you have to say. With time, patience, and practice you will be able to control your mind and those of others in any situation.

Finally, if you found this book useful in any way, a review on Amazon is always appreciated!

99

9 781720 429678